Pet Project

by Christine Peymani

Bath · New York · Singapore · Hong Kong · Cologne · Delhi · Melbourne

First published by Parragon in 2007
Parragon
Queen Street House
4 Queen Street
Bath BA1 1HE, UK

www.bratz.com
TM & © MGA Entertainment, Inc.
"Bratz", and all related logos, names,
characters and distinctive likenesses are the
exclusive property of MGA Entertainment, Inc.
All Rights Reserved. Used under license by Parragon.

ISBN 978-1-4054-8738-2

Printed in china

CHAPTER 1

"Aww, what a sweetie!" Jade exclaimed.

She was crouching in front of a cage in the Stilesville Pet Shelter, patting the head of a cute black-and-white puppy. Even though Jade was much more of a cat person—her friends even called her 'Kool Kat'—she was totally charmed by the little guy.

"Ooh, he is cute," Yasmin agreed. But she hardly glanced up from the adorable, fluffy white puppy whose ears she was petting.

"Hmm, looks like you've already found the puppy you want," Jade said with a grin, joining her best friend at the fluffy dog's cage.

"Well..." Yasmin began slowly. "I mean, I want to give all the puppies a fair chance, and the one you were petting is really cute, too. But my parents said I could only have one, so I have to choose sometime." She looked around at all the other dogs with their noses pressed against the bars of their cages, yipping anxiously to get the girls' attention. "It's just so hard to pick!"

"I know," Jade replied. "It's really sad seeing them all in cages like this. But Yasmin, you don't have to rescue all of them. I'm sure someone else will adopt these other dogs."

"Do you really think so?" Yasmin asked anxiously.

"Absolutely," Jade insisted. "I mean, look how cute they all are! How could they not find new homes?"

Just then, the puppy Yasmin was petting slurped her hand enthusiastically, making her giggle.

"I think that puppy has made the decision for you!" Jade exclaimed.

"I do like her..." Yasmin beamed.

The dog yipped excitedly.

"I think she likes you too!" Jade added, leaning down to pat the dog's head. Then she stood up and went to find one of the shelter employees. "Let's get your new puppy out of that cage!"

A lady from the shelter brought Yasmin all the adoption paperwork, and soon she had the fuzzy, wriggling puppy cuddled up in her arms.

"What are you gonna name her?" Jade asked, giggling as the puppy slurped Yasmin's face.

"Well..." Yasmin looked at her puppy thoughtfully. "What about Aspen? You know, because she's as white and fluffy as freshly fallen snow?"

"I love it!" Jade cried. "You are so creative."

"Well, naming characters is my favorite part of being a writer," Yasmin told her friend.

Yasmin was constantly writing, and all her friends were sure she would be a famous novelist someday.

"Come on, we've got to introduce Aspen to the rest of the girls!" Jade declared.

Jade and Yasmin hurried out to the car, where they settled Aspen in a pet carrier in the backseat. Yasmin hopped behind the wheel while Jade speed-dialed their other two best friends, Sasha and Cloe.

"Are you guys finished with your study group yet?" Jade asked. "Because we have something exciting to show you! Be at Yasmin's in fifteen." She flipped her phone shut and told

Yasmin, "They're on their way!"

"I wish they could've come with us to pick out my new puppy," Yasmin said. "But I'm so glad you were there with me—you were such a huge help!"

"Wouldn't have missed it, Pretty Princess," Jade replied.

Yasmin's friends called her 'Pretty Princess' because she was always so graceful and quietly confident that she seemed almost regal.

Yasmin had just

pulled into her driveway when Cloe's cruiser swung in behind her.

"Perfect timing!" Yasmin exclaimed.

"Quick, you take Aspen inside and get her ready to meet the girls," Jade suggested. "I'll distract them for a minute so you can get her settled first."

"Good plan," Yasmin agreed. She grabbed the pet carrier and darted inside.

"Hey, where's Yas going in such a hurry?" Sasha asked as she got out of the car.

"Oh, she had something she needed to take care of real quick," Jade explained. "So, how was the study group?"

"Long," Cloe sighed. "Who knew there was so much to learn about the entire history of the world?"

"Not the entire history," Sasha interrupted. "Just Ancient Rome through the founding of

America. There are, like, thousands of years we aren't being tested on."

"Wait, this is all for one test?" Jade asked.

"Well, yeah, but it is our final," Sasha explained. "Mrs. Ackerman just likes to be thorough."

"I'm never going to remember all that stuff!" Cloe complained.

"Well, Yasmin and I have just the thing to cheer you up," Jade told her. "Come on inside."

"Ooh, yeah, what's the big surprise?" Cloe asked, her history worries forgotten.

"You'll have to see for yourself!" Jade said, leading her friends into the house.

The girls gasped when they spotted Yasmin sitting on the couch with her puppy perched on her lap.

"I didn't know you were getting a dog!"

Sasha cried, running over to pet the puppy.

"My parents just decided I could," Yasmin explained, "so I wanted to rescue one as soon as possible."

She noticed that Cloe was hanging back, looking kind of bummed.

"Cloe, what's wrong?" Yasmin asked. "Don't you like my new puppy?"

"She's fine," Cloe replied with a shrug.

"Her name is Aspen," Jade added. "Isn't that a cool name?"

"Totally!" Sasha agreed, but Cloe didn't say anything.

Yasmin handed Aspen to Sasha and walked over to Cloe, putting her arm around her best friend.

"Angel, what's wrong?" she murmured. Cloe was known as 'Angel' because she was always so sweet, plus she was always putting together looks that were totally heavenly.

Cloe gazed at her friend sadly, then blurted out, "I can't believe you got a new puppy without me!"

"I know, I really wish you could've been there with me," Yasmin replied. "But I didn't want this poor puppy to have to stay at the shelter any longer than she had to."

"Oh I know, I didn't mean that you should've left sweet little Aspen at the shelter," Cloe cried. "I know I'm being totally selfish! But it's just that we usually share everything, and this is pretty huge!"

"But Cloe, that's why I wanted you to be here as soon as I brought Aspen home," Yasmin explained.

Cloe still looked upset, then Aspen scurried up to them, her big furry paws slipping on the hardwood floors.

"Aww!" Cloe cooed. She leaned over to scoop Aspen up.

"Look, she knows how great you are already!" Yasmin exclaimed.

"Well...I think she's pretty great, too," Cloe replied grudgingly. "She's definitely the right puppy for you."

"As soon as I saw her, I knew you'd love her," Yasmin said.

"I really do." Cloe said, nuzzling the puppy.

Sasha and Jade crowded in to pet Aspen too. The puppy

©MGA

yipped happily, thrilled by all the attention.

"You know, this totally makes me want to get a pet, too," said Cloe.

"Ooh, you should!" Yasmin cried. "Then our puppies could play together!"

"Let's go to the pet shelter right now!" Cloe exclaimed.

"Um, Angel, I think it's closed," Jade said.

"Well then, I'm going there first thing in the morning!" Cloe declared.

"Cloe, you're not exactly a morning person," Sasha pointed out.

"Okay fine," Cloe replied. "First thing in the afternoon, then."

"Sounds good," Sasha agreed. "But for now, let's make Aspen feel at home. Yasmin, do you have puppy supplies?"

"Yep," Yasmin told her. "I have a comfy doggy bed in my room for her, plus some puppy toys. There's puppy chow and water in the kitchen. Ooh, and I got her an adorable sparkly collar and matching leash!"

"You are so prepared!" Jade exclaimed. "Okay, let's get this puppy fully accessorized!"

Cloe handed Aspen over to Yasmin, and the girls hurried into Yasmin's room. When Cloe set the dog down in her new bed, Aspen rolled around happily, her tongue hanging out in a big puppy smile.

Sasha picked up the cute heart-shaped chew toy that Yasmin had left in the dog bed for Aspen.

"Hey, girl, do you wanna play?"

Aspen leapt up and grabbed the toy, shaking her head as she tried to pull it away from Sasha.

"How cute!"

Sasha let go of the toy and Aspen ran

across the room with it hanging from her mouth, looking very proud of herself.

"Wow, you sure know how to make a puppy happy," Cloe told Yasmin.

"I hope she'll like her collar, too," Yasmin replied. She picked up a rhinestone-studded black collar from her bedside table and fastened it around the dog's neck. Aspen looked up at her curiously, pawed at the collar for a second, then sat up straight, turning her head from side to side as though showing off her new accessory.

"What a diva!" Jade declared.

"She's definitely a posh pooch," Sasha agreed. "I think she'll fit right in here!"

"Yeah, she's totally perfect," Cloe added as they all gathered around to pet their newest, furriest friend.

CHAPTER 2

"Guys, I was up all night," Cloe declared the next day, collapsing dramatically on Sasha's bed.

The girls had met up at Sasha's place for their usual Saturday shopping trip, but Cloe looked way too exhausted to hit the mall.

"Me too!" Yasmin exclaimed, perching on the edge of the bed next to her friend. "But I was up with a new puppy—what's your excuse?"

"I just kept thinking about the animal shelter and how it's full of sweet little pets just like Aspen, all trapped in cages and lonely, and I got so upset that I just couldn't sleep," Cloe explained. "So I went over to the shelter first thing in the morning, and the cats and dogs all looked so cute and sad that I wanted to cry."

"Cloe, you can't let yourself get all worked up like that," Sasha said. She was curled up in a big, cushy armchair that she kept in her room for just such hangout occasions. "I mean, I feel really bad for those little guys too, but I'm sure they'll find awesome owners just like Aspen did."

"But what if they don't?" Cloe wailed. "What if they get stuck spending their entire lives in those tiny cages?"

"We just have

to hope that doesn't happen," Jade said from her spot on the floor, where she sat cross-legged on one of Sasha's comfy floor cushions.

Cloe sat up straight and leaned toward her friends eagerly. "This may sound crazy, but I really think there's a lot more we can do."

"Okay, 'this may sound crazy' is not necessarily the best way to start," Sasha replied.

"Come on, let me finish!" Cloe insisted. She paused for effect, then continued, "Well, at first I thought I would just adopt all of the animals from the shelter."

"Cloe!" her best friends cried in unison.

"How could you possibly take care of that many animals?" Jade demanded.

"I thought of that," Cloe admitted. "But then I figured it's got to be better than being trapped at the shelter."

"Cloe, that's nuts," Sasha declared. "And there's no way your parents would ever go for it."

"Look, if you really want to help those animals, why not just volunteer at the shelter?" Yasmin suggested.

"I'd love to, but I feel like I have to do something bigger than that," Cloe insisted. "But you're right that it doesn't make sense to adopt them all myself. I mean, that's way too many pets!"

"I can't stand the suspense," Jade interrupted. "Come on, tell us your big plan!"

"Well, I decided that if I can't adopt them all myself, I am going to personally find a new home for every one of those pets," Cloe replied.

She sat back with a huge, self-satisfied smile on her face.

"Well, that sounds a little more reasonable," Sasha replied. "But how exactly do you plan to do that?"

"That's where you girls come in," Cloe explained. "We're going to start an adopt-an-animal campaign and by the time we're through, every man, woman, and fashionista in Stilesville is going to have a brand-new adopted pet at home."

"I like it," Sasha agreed. "Okay, first we need to talk to the people who run the shelter and find out what they've tried already, and get them on board."

"Ooh, and we should come up with some sort of signature event to really get people excited!" Jade added. "I am all about planning happening events."

"Totally," Yasmin agreed. "And once people see all those cute kitties and puppies, they won't be able to resist taking one home!"

"You guys are the coolest!" Cloe exclaimed. "I knew I could count on you to help me make this happen."

"Absolutely," Jade replied. "But I take it this means we won't be hitting the mall today?"

"Jade, the animals have to come first!" Cloe cried.

"Angel, I was totally kidding," Jade told her friend.

"Oh," Cloe said, looking embarrassed. "I knew that."

Jade shook her head at her friend, grinning. Cloe frequently got so caught up in her ideas that she lost track of everything else—which sometimes included her sense of humor. It always came back quickly, though.

"Come on, girls, let's hit the animal shelter!" Sasha declared. As the organizer of the group, she was always encouraging the other girls to stay on track.

When they showed up at the shelter, Sasha asked to speak to whoever was in charge. The shelter's director, Ms. Fiske, came out, and the girls introduced themselves.

"Weren't you girls just in here adopting a dog?" she asked Yasmin and Jade.

Yasmin started to answer, but before she could, Cloe jumped in and exclaimed, "Yeah, and that's totally what inspired me to help all these other animals!"

Yasmin looked annoyed, but didn't say anything.

"Well, I think that's very sweet of you," Ms. Fiske replied. "So what did you have in mind?"

"We wanted to know what you'd already tried," Sasha explained.

"Because we're all about coming up with totally original ideas," Jade added.

"Honestly, we could use some original ideas," Ms. Fiske admitted. "We're so busy taking care of these animals that we don't really have much opportunity to get the word out. I mean, we hold adoption events around town when we can, but we usually just set up in the park and hope people come by. Nothing too fancy."

"Well, we are known for our fancy events," Jade declared. "In fact, I'm picturing a high-class pet show to showcase all these adorable, adoptable animals. We'll give them all makeovers to have them looking their absolute best."

"Ooh, and we could offer lots of different prizes, like 'Best Tail-Wagger' and 'Funniest' and 'Most Cuddly', so all the pets could win an award," Yasmin suggested. "That way, everyone could adopt a champion!"

"Awesome idea. I'll design the ribbons,"

Jade offered. "And make sure the pet show is the event of the year, of course!"

"And I'll make some totally eye-catching posters to get people excited about the event," Cloe added.

"I could do a write-up for the school newspaper," Yasmin suggested. "And I bet I could get the town newspaper editor to let me do a piece for him, too. I mean, I already wrote some stuff for him over the summer."

"Perfect!" Sasha agreed. "And I'll announce it on the school radio station, and I'm sure the local station will pick it up too—I have an 'in' since I did that internship there."

"And don't forget the school TV station," Yasmin reminded them. "We'll include it in our morning announcements. Plus the local TV station still loves us from when we guest hosted their morning show, so I know they'll help us get the word out."

"Wow, you girls are full of great ideas!" Ms. Fiske exclaimed. "And you certainly are well-connected. I'm thrilled that you're so eager to help."

"Anything for these sweet little animals," Cloe replied.

"Now we just have to figure out where to hold the show," Jade continued.

Sasha gazed thoughtfully at the worn-down looking shelter. "I think we should have it right here."

"I don't know—" Jade protested, but Sasha interrupted her.

"I know it needs some work, but don't you think a makeover would be the perfect way to make these pets more comfortable until they find new homes?" Sasha asked.

"I do love a makeover," Jade admitted.

"Ooh, it'd be so much fun to draw up designs for the new and improved shelter!" Cloe squealed.

"And it would really help drive awareness of the shelter if we held a fabulous event right here," Yasmin added.

"Well, we would love that," Ms. Fiske interjected. "We've been wanting to redo the shelter for years, but we never had the money for it."

"Yeah, Sasha, how are we going to pay for all this?" Yasmin asked.

"I've got a few ideas," Sasha replied, her eyes sparkling. She was never happier than when she had something new to plan, and she always came up with innovative ways to make even their wildest ideas work.

They said goodbye to Ms. Fiske, then headed back to Sasha's to hash out their plans.

"Yasmin, are there any truly hip pet magazines out there?" Sasha asked.

"Sure—Bowwow Meow Magazine is the coolest pet mag on the market," Yasmin replied. "Why?"

"Because we're going to get them to sponsor this event!" Sasha announced.

"And how exactly are we going to do that, Bunny Boo?" Jade wanted to know. Sasha's friends called her 'Bunny Boo' because she was totally into the urban scene—plus she seemed to have unlimited supplies of energy!

"Oh, you'll see," Sasha replied mysteriously. Her friends raised their eyebrows, but let it go at that—Sasha did have a way of making great things happen.

"I think we'll need about two weeks to get everything together," Sasha declared once they had all settled back into her bedroom.

"No way!" Cloe cried. "I am not leaving those poor little pets in there for that long!"

"But Cloe, we have to line up a sponsor, and get the word out, and makeover all the pets, plus redo the whole shelter," Yasmin reminded her. "That's going to take some time, don't you think?"

"Okay..." Cloe said reluctantly. She crossed her arms and added, "But I don't have to like it!"

"Noted," Jade said with a laugh.

"So what are the first steps, Sasha?" Yasmin asked.

"I'm glad you asked!" Sasha replied. She

pulled out her laptop and started briskly typing a to-do list. She was crazy about to-do lists! "First, we need a name for the event to totally set the tone." She turned to stare expectantly at Yasmin.

"What?" Yasmin asked.

"Pretty Princess, you are our resident writer," Cloe replied. "Names are kind of your thing."

"True," Yasmin admitted. She looked thoughtful for a moment. "Well, what about the Precious Paws Pet Show?"

"That's adorable!" Jade exclaimed.

"See, that's why we depend on you for this sort of thing," Sasha added.

Yasmin blushed. "Really, it was nothing. I'll keep coming up with ideas."

"No, Yas, that's perfect!" Cloe insisted. She pulled out her sketchbook and sketched a cool paw-print logo with a diamond-studded look. "See, then we can use this logo on everything!"

"Cloe, that looks so good!" Jade exclaimed. "I'll design the prize ribbons using that logo, too."

Cloe kept sketching, and soon had a rough poster idea to show the girls, which they all loved. Sasha was making a list of all the supplies they'd need to makeover the pets and the shelter. Jade started planning a color scheme for the event—bright pink and black looked perfect to her—and Yasmin was busy jotting down all sorts of prizes they could give out to all the animals.

"Do you girls want to stay over tonight, so we can keep planning?" Sasha asked.

"Sure!" Cloe and Jade exclaimed, but Yasmin looked uncertain.

"I really should get home to Aspen," she

said. "My parents were watching her today, but she's my puppy. I can't make them take care of her all night."

"I totally understand," Sasha replied.

"Does anyone want to come help me out tonight?" Yasmin asked. "She was pretty restless last night, and I could use the company."

"Oh, I think the rest of us had better stay here and work on this pet show," Cloe said distractedly. "But we'll see you tomorrow, okay? Have fun with your puppy!"

Yasmin gave each of her best friends a quick goodbye hug, then hurried out of the room, trying not to let them see how hurt she felt. The girls were already totally engrossed in their own projects again before she had even closed the door behind her.

CHAPTER 3

When Yasmin got home, Aspen ran to the door to meet her, jumping up and down and yipping excitedly.

"Aww, did you miss me, little sweetie?" she asked. She scooped up her puppy and giggled as Aspen licked her face. "You're such a good girl, aren't you?"

She carried Aspen into her room and settled the puppy onto her bed.

"Man, am I tired!" Yasmin exclaimed. "My friends and I were busy all day long coming up with ways to rescue your furry friends from the shelter. Doesn't that sound cool?"

"Woof!" Aspen agreed, making Yasmin laugh. Yasmin changed into her cute new striped pajamas and crawled into bed with her dog nestled beside her.

"I'm so glad I adopted you," Yasmin sighed as she drifted off to sleep. "You're the best friend a girl could ever have."

But it was only a few hours later when Aspen woke her up, whimpering loudly and scratching at the door.

"Wha–what is it?" Yasmin murmured groggily. "Oh–Aspen. Do you need to go out, sweetie?"

Aspen peered up at Yasmin, her big brown eyes wide, and barked insistently.

©MGA

"Okay, okay, let's go outside."

Yasmin pulled on a robe and slid her feet into her fuzzy slippers, then headed for the back yard with her puppy.

When they got outside, Aspen wanted to play. She grabbed her pink ball, which Yasmin's parents had left in the yard, and brought it to Yasmin.

"It's too late for playing, Aspen," Yasmin explained. "We'll play tomorrow, okay?" But the little dog looked so sad that Yasmin took the ball and tossed it. "But just this once," she added.

Aspen bounded across the yard and carried the ball back to Yasmin, her tail wagging rapidly as she waited for Yasmin to throw it again.

"Come on, let's go inside," Yasmin insisted. She took the ball and headed back inside with Aspen following eagerly behind her.

Back in the house, Aspen spotted her food dish and forgot all about the ball. There was still some puppy chow left from earlier in the day, and she chomped happily on it.

"Aspen, let's get back to bed," Yasmin called, stifling a yawn. But her puppy ignored her, lapping up some water instead. "Aspen, come!" Yasmin demanded, and even though Aspen hadn't exactly learned commands yet, she looked up at the stern tone in her owner's voice, then obediently trotted after her and back into the bedroom.

"Sleep well, Aspen," Yasmin said as she and her dog curled up in bed again. "I'll see you in the morning."

But her new dog woke her up three more times that night, so by the next morning, when her doorbell rang and woke her up again, Yasmin was totally fed up. She stomped to the door and threw it open, letting it bang against the wall.

"What?" she asked.

"Oh—hey Yasmin," Cloe said, looking at her friend worriedly. "Is everything okay?"

"Actually, everything is not okay," Yasmin snapped. "I've been up all night with my new puppy because, thanks to your crazy scheme, no one had time to help me with her."

"Yas, she's your puppy," Cloe replied. "I mean, you kind of have to take care of her yourself, don't you think?"

"But you guys could've helped me this weekend if you hadn't had to steal the spotlight like you always do," Yasmin shouted. "I mean, everyone was all excited that I adopted a new dog, so suddenly you want to adopt every dog in the entire shelter? Why can't you ever let me have the spotlight for just one minute?"

"Let's talk this through," Cloe begged. "Yasmin, please let me in."

"I don't know if I feel like talking to you right now," Yasmin replied. She turned on her heel and stalked back to her room with Cloe trailing after her.

Yasmin slumped onto her bed with her arms crossed over her chest.

"Well? What did you want to say?" she demanded.

"You're just tired," Cloe began. "Look, I'm sorry Aspen kept you up all night, but she probably would've done that even if I'd been here, don't you think?"

"Maybe..." Yasmin murmured uncertainly.

"Hey, why don't I take Aspen for a walk so you can take a nap?" Cloe offered.

"That is exactly the kind of thing you could've helped me with last night," Yasmin complained. "I mean, of course she's my responsibility, but I thought we were supposed to help each other through everything!"

"Of course we are!" Cloe replied. "That's what best friends are for. But I thought rescuing other animals like Aspen was helping."

"Humph," Yasmin said, rolling over on her bed so her back was turned to Cloe.

Cloe stared at her friend sadly for a moment, then

announced, "Okay, I'm going to take Aspen for that walk. I'll see you when you wake up."

She clipped Aspen's leash to her collar and strode outside, walking fast as though trying to outrun Yasmin's accusations.

"Aspen, you don't think she's right, do you?" Cloe asked the puppy, who was trotting happily at her side, pausing to sniff at flowers and trees as they made their way down the street. "I wasn't trying to take all of the focus off you. I'm excited about you! I just wanted some of the focus on me."

Cloe gasped and stopped walking, pulling Aspen to a halt beside her.

"Oh my gosh, Yasmin is totally right!" She put her hands over her mouth, mortified, while the puppy stared up at her. "I was jealous that she had such a cool new pet, so I tried to one-up her!"

"Woof! Woof!" Aspen replied, and Cloe

smiled down at the dog.

"You're right, girl," Cloe declared. "I've got to go apologize to your owner right away."

Cloe hurried back to her best friend's house with Aspen running alongside her. She burst into Yasmin's room just as her friend was awakening from a nap.

"I'm so sorry!" Cloe exclaimed, rushing over to give Yasmin a hug.

"Wha−?" Yasmin asked drowsily, blinking her eyes rapidly as she fought off sleep. Aspen leapt onto the bed and licked her owner's cheek, making Yasmin giggle as she stroked her puppy's head.

"You were totally right, Pretty Princess," Cloe announced. "I was trying to steal the spotlight, and I'm sorry. But I do want to help the other homeless animals, and I do need your help to do it. Please, will you help us plan the pet show some more today?"

"Cloe, I told you, I have to take care of Aspen–" Yasmin began, but Cloe cut her off.

"I know, I know, but I thought we could all meet over here," Cloe explained. "And then if Aspen needed anything, we could all take turns taking care of her. Just like you wanted, right?"

"I guess that could work…" Yasmin replied slowly, but Cloe seized on her response excitedly.

"Awesome! I'll call the girls!" Cloe exclaimed.

"Okay," Yasmin agreed. She looked at Cloe solemnly. "But Cloe?"

"What is it, Yas?" Cloe asked worriedly, certain her friend was still angry with her.

"Could I possibly sneak in a few more minutes of naptime while we wait for the others? I really didn't sleep all night."

Yasmin's eyes were already drooping closed again.

"Absolutely!" Cloe cried, relieved. "Aspen and I will go play in the living room until the girls get here. And we'll be really quiet, I swear!"

"Thanks, Cloe," Yasmin murmured, already falling back to sleep. "You're a good friend."

A wide grin spread across Cloe's face. "You too, Yas," she said happily.

She led Aspen out of the room and shut the door softly behind her. Once she had settled onto the couch with the puppy beside her, she speed-dialed Jade and Sasha to announce that Yasmin's house would be pet-show-planning central today.

CHAPTER 4

On Monday morning, it was finally time to translate all that planning into action. It was also the last week of school, which meant it was time for Sasha and Cloe to conquer their History final.

"How can Mrs. Ackerman expect us to know all of this?" Cloe moaned, reviewing her notes with Sasha in the school commons before the bell rang.

"It is what we've been studying all year, Angel," Sasha reminded her. But Cloe just sighed and paged through her notes frantically.

"What are you looking for?" Sasha asked.

"Oh, I don't know...just the key to all historical facts and figures—some magical solution that will help me ace this test," Cloe declared. "Because short of that, I think I'm in big trouble."

"We probably should've spent more time this weekend studying instead of planning the pet show," Sasha agreed. The first bell rang, signaling that it was time to get to class. "But I'm sure we'll be okay."

The girls gathered up their notebooks and pens, shoved them in their backpacks, and jetted to their classroom. They slid into their seats just as the second bell rang, narrowly avoiding tardy marks.

"Okay, class, let's get started," Mrs. Ackerman called. "You'll have the entire class period to finish this test."

Cloe and Sasha exchanged a nervous look.

"Good luck," Sasha whispered.

"You too," Cloe replied.

Their teacher passed out copies of the test, and the girls, along with the rest of their classmates, were immediately engrossed in the history of the world.

When the bell rang, Cloe and Sasha both nearly jumped out of their seats.

"Pass your tests up!" Mrs. Ackerman said.

The girls handed their tests to the students

in front of them, then bolted for the door. In the hallway, they met up with Jade and Yasmin.

"Well, how'd the big test go?" Yasmin asked.

"Don't wanna talk about it," Cloe muttered.

"Ooh, that bad?" Jade turned to Sasha to get the scoop.

"It wasn't easy," Sasha admitted. "But at least it's over!"

"And now we can really get our pet-show promotions in gear," Yasmin reminded the others.

"Does everyone have their assignments?" Sasha asked, whipping out her planner and scanning her to-do list.

"You and I will get to work on the school coverage in our journalism class next period," Yasmin began. "And I'm sure Mr. Mazzei will let us call the local media outlets during class."

"That's when I'll hit up Bowwow Meow

Magazine, too," Sasha added.

"I'll finalize my poster design in art class next hour," Cloe said "I really want to get Mr. Del Rio's input on it."

"And I'll work on the prize ribbons in home ec," Jade interjected. "We're doing a sewing unit right now, and I know Ms. Shepard has a ton of gorgeous ribbons stashed away with her sewing supplies."

"All right girls, break!" Sasha cried. The girls gave each other high-fives, then dashed off to their classes.

In their journalism class, Yasmin and Sasha explained their plan to Mr. Mazzei. He agreed that Yasmin should do a cover story for the school paper on the Stilesville Animal Shelter's efforts to help homeless animals, and on the upcoming Precious Paws Pet Show.

"This will be the paper's last issue of the school year," Mr. Mazzei reminded her, "so that's a pretty important cover spot to get."

"I really appreciate it," Yasmin replied, "and I'm sure if all those poor abandoned pets could read, they'd appreciate it too!"

Yasmin got to work researching the shelter, calling up Ms. Fiske to get additional facts.

Sasha convinced her teacher to let her do a 'Pet Spotlight' segment on the school's TV station all week.

"I'll bring on a cute, cuddly cat or dog that will be featured in our pet show and tell everyone about his or her background," she explained. "Hopefully people will be clamoring to adopt the little sweetie by the end of the day!"

"Sounds like fun," Mr. Mazzei agreed. Sasha called the shelter and got ideas for four pets that would be perfect to profile. She made arrangements to pick each one up the morning before the show, then return them during her second-period journalism class.

"Mr. Mazzei, can we promote the event on the school's radio station, too?" Sasha asked after she hung up the phone.

"Sure," he agreed. "It sounds like you girls are all over this event, so I know it'll be a huge success!"

Next, Yasmin called the local paper and spoke to the editor there, Mr. Siegel.

"This is such an important event, and having coverage of it in your paper would be such a huge help," she told him.

"It sounds interesting," Mr. Siegel agreed. "And I did like the pieces you did for me over the summer. So what would it be, a write-up of the event?"

"Well, I'd like to start with a profile of the shelter and how we're making it over to make it more comfortable for the pets and more appealing for prospective pet owners," Yasmin said. "Then, I'd love to do a follow-up covering the event itself, to help drive traffic to the shelter even after the pet show is over."

"That sounds good," Mr. Siegel told her. "We're always looking for community service events to cover—and what you girls are doing definitely sounds like a service to the community! We can run the first piece this weekend, and the second one the Monday after the pet show."

"Thank you so much!" Yasmin squealed. "I promise, I won't let you down!"

She couldn't wait to tell Sasha about her awesome new assignment, but when she ran over to her friend's side, Sasha was still on the phone to a producer at the local TV station.

"It'll be like Extreme Pet Shelter Makeover," Sasha explained. "The footage will be truly incredible. And then a segment on the pet show, showing off all these cute little critters on the runway. I mean, who wouldn't watch that?"

"It does sound pretty amazing," the producer, Ms. Clark, replied. "If you and your friends will come on our show and talk as enthusiastically about your project as you did just now, we'd be happy to have you do a couple of segments."

"Awesome!" Sasha replied. "We're starting on the shelter makeover today, so if you want to send out a cameraman this afternoon, there'll be plenty of cool stuff going on!"

"Will do," Ms. Clark agreed. "I'll try to drop in too."

"Great!" Sasha replied. She hung up, and she and Yasmin turned to each other, both jumping up and down in excitement.

MY DOG ROCKS

©MGA

"The TV station's gonna cover it! And we get to be on the show!" Sasha squealed.

"The newspaper's covering it too! And I get to write the articles!" Yasmin added.

"Yay!" the girls exclaimed, giving each other a quick hug.

They noticed their classmates staring at them, and Sasha asked, "What? We're just excited about saving some animals!"

The other students smiled and shook their heads—those girls were always planning something big!

"Okay, back to my research," Yasmin said. "Just wanted to share my news."

"And I've still gotta call the Stilesville radio station," Sasha replied.

She called the station and explained about all the coverage they had already, and the producer agreed to have all of the DJs hype the event.

"Plus we'd love to have you girls on the day of the pet show to talk about everything you're doing," the producer, Ms. Leland, added. "This is a fabulous human-interest piece!"

"Perfect!" Sasha agreed.

She jotted down the date and time of the interview in her planner. Between the TV shows, radio programs, and newspaper stories, she and her best friends were going to be pretty busy promoting this event.

Sasha dashed over to the computer next to Yasmin's and looked up Bowwow Meow Magazine.

"These are the big guys," Sasha announced. "If we can get them on board, it'll be smooth sailing on this event!"

"You should talk to the managing editor if you can," Yasmin told her friend. "She's the one who can really make the call."

"Good tip," Sasha replied. "Are you sure you don't want to talk to her?"

"No, I think you should handle it," Yasmin said with a laugh. "I mean, you can convince anyone of anything!"

"That is my specialty," Sasha admitted. "Okay, I'm on it." She dialed the number from the magazine's website and asked for the managing editor.

"Hello, Ms. Tanaka?" she asked when the editor came on the line. "My name is Sasha and I'm with the Stilesville Animal Shelter's first annual Precious Paws Pet Show. To launch this event, we'll be doing a complete remodel of the shelter, plus makeovers for all of the cats and dogs currently housed there to prepare them for the show. This gala event will be held next Saturday."

"Sounds interesting," Ms. Tanaka replied.

"But we need several months' notice to include something in our magazine."

"Oh, I understand that you can't feature the event in advance," Sasha replied. "We were actually hoping that you might be interested in sponsoring the event. Obviously we'd promote the magazine in all of our news coverage, which includes newspaper, radio, and TV outlets. In return, your publication would be associated with a truly spectacular event that will help a lot of animals."

"What would you need from us?" Ms. Tanaka asked.

"Mostly just paint and pet supplies to take the pet shelter from blah to beautiful," Sasha explained.

"Well, we do get a lot of supplies sent to us by companies hoping we'll cover their products," Ms. Tanaka began. "I could send you a ton of pet beds and blankets, plus toys, collars, and food dishes. All top of the line. Would that help?"

"Absolutely!" Sasha exclaimed. "Does that mean you'll help us out?"

"Only if we can feature the 'Precious Paws Best in Show' winner on the cover of our magazine, along with a feature about the event," Ms. Tanaka answered.

"That would be fabulous!" Sasha cried.

"Glad you like the idea," Ms. Tanaka said. "I've got to get to an editorial meeting, but I'll make sure that a check for the makeover and a batch of pet supplies go out to you today."

"You're never gonna believe this!" Sasha told Yasmin after she hung up the phone. She recounted her awesome conversation with Bowwow Meow's editor, and soon she and Yasmin were squealing again.

"I really think we're going to find homes for

every single pet in the shelter, just like Cloe wanted," Yasmin declared.

"You know, I think we just might," Sasha agreed with a smile.

CHAPTER 5

When the girls met up at their usual table in the school cafeteria, Sasha and Yasmin were bursting with good news. The girls all set down their trays, then started dishing.

"This pet show is gonna be a huge hit!" Cloe announced after her friends told her all about the media coverage plus their super-cool sponsorship.

Jade pulled a handful of gorgeous hot pink, teal, and bright purple ribbons out of her bag and showed them to the girls. "Since we want every pet to be a winner, I wanted to mix up the typical blue, red and white ribbon color scheme a little," she explained. "Plus, I think these are so much more eye-catching!"

"Totally," Yasmin gushed. "The pets are all

going to look absolutely adorable with those ribbons on their collars!"

"Thanks, Yas," Jade replied. "And Ms. Shepard has the whole class helping with them, so we'll have enough for every single puppy and kitten. Then, after those are finished, she said everyone's final project can be making cute cushions for all the animals! We were going to do pillows anyway, and everyone was happy to donate theirs."

"That's so nice of your teacher—and your classmates," Sasha replied.

"Well, she's a huge pet lover," Jade told her friends. "Oh, and she said we could have any fabric we wanted for the shelter makeover."

"That's awesome," Cloe said. "So here's what I worked on with Mr. Del

©MGA

Rio." She pulled out a glossy poster and continued, "He thought we needed an event mascot, and I knew just the pooch to pull it off."

She unrolled the poster and showed it to the girls. On a hot-pink, polka-dotted background, it featured the sparkly paw-print logo Cloe had designed, all the details about the event, and a drawing of Aspen right in the middle.

"Since she's the one who started the whole thing, I thought Aspen should get to take center stage," Cloe explained.

"Angel, you drew her so perfectly!" Yasmin cried. "I love it!"

"So you don't mind if we make your puppy our Precious Paws mascot?" Cloe asked, her eyes twinkling. "You don't think it'll go to her head, or anything?"

"I think I can keep her ego in check,"

Yasmin replied, giggling.

"That looks great, Cloe," Sasha agreed. "But don't forget to add the Bowwow Meow logo." Turning to Jade, she added, "And we'll need a special 'Best in Show' ribbon for our grand prize winner to wear on the cover of the magazine."

Out of nowhere, they were interrupted by their two least-favorite people—Kaycee and Kirstee, a pair of seriously mean twins the girls called the Tweevils.

"What's that?" Kirstee demanded. "You girls are gonna be on the cover of Bowwow Magazine? Kind of insulting to the dogs, don't you think?"

"It's Bowwow Meow, and it's a pet from the Stilesville Shelter that will be featured on the cover," Yasmin replied coldly.

"That's my favorite pet magazine!" Kaycee squealed.

"So why is such a hip magazine showing off some mutt?" Kirstee asked.

"The adorable cat or dog who wins Best in Show at the Precious Paws Pet Show is getting the cover spot," Sasha explained, "because the magazine, unlike some people I won't mention, actually cares about helping the less fortunate."

"Ooh, Kirstee, we have to enter our puppies in that pet show!" Kaycee cried. "Can we, can we, can we?"

"I don't care what you do," Kirstee snapped. "But it would be pretty awesome if Muffy and Buffy got to be on the cover of the hottest pet magazine in the country."

"I bet it would launch their pet modeling career!" Kaycee exclaimed. "We'd get tons of dog food and pooper-scooper endorsement deals!"

"Not to burst your pooper-scooper dreams,

but this show is for pets from the shelter only," Jade interrupted.

"That's totally discriminatory!" Kirstee protested.

"No, it isn't," Cloe shouted. "This is a charity event to help homeless pets find new homes, not to help your spoiled dogs feel special."

"They're purebreds," Kaycee announced. "That means you have to spoil them!"

"Well, whatever they are, they still can't be in the show," Sasha replied. "Now if you'll excuse us, we've got a lot of work to do here."

"I hope you're working on a new wardrobe," Kirstee said snidely. "I'd have to say that's your real problem area." Turning to her twin sister, she added, "Come on, Kaycee, let's get out of here before someone sees us with these losers and thinks we actually like them!"

The twins burst out into high-pitched, totally obnoxious giggles as they stalked away.

"Somebody should put them in a cage," Jade grumbled.

"They're just mad because Miffy and Biffy or whatever their names are will never be famous," Cloe replied. Pointing to her poster, she added, "Certainly nowhere near as famous as Aspen here!"

"And that's as it should be," Sasha declared.

The girls' friends Vinessa and Meygan strolled over and stopped to check out the dazzling ribbons and brightly colored poster spread out on their lunch table.

"What are you ladies up to now?" Meygan asked.

"Just making over the local animal shelter and finding a new home for every stray pet in

Stilesville," Cloe told her. "What about you?"

"Wow, nothing as exciting as all that!" Vinessa replied. "Do you need any help?"

"Do we ever," Jade said with a laugh. "We have to redo the whole shelter, plan our TV and radio spots, and get all the pets looking totally glam. Oh yeah, and study for the rest of our finals. You want in?"

"For sure!" Meygan and Vinessa chorused.

"Do you think we should recruit the boys too, in case we need help building something?" Cloe asked shyly.

"Yeah, why don't you go see if Cameron is interested?" Sasha teased. Cloe and Cameron were totally into each other, but neither of them would ever admit it.

"I—I didn't mean Cameron," Cloe stammered. "I mean—I was talking about all the boys."

"Of course you were, Cloe," Jade teased. "So why don't you find out if all the boys want to help?"

"No problem," Cloe agreed, blushing. She strolled over to the boys' table and casually asked if any of them wanted to help with an event at the local pet shelter.

"Sure, Cloe," Cameron replied shyly. "You know I love animals."

"Yeah, count me in," Dylan added.

"Me too!" Koby chimed in.

"You guys are the best!" Cloe exclaimed. She tried not to look at Cam as she continued, "So I'll see you all after school today?"

"We're there!" Dylan answered for all of them.

"Well girls, do you think nine is enough volunteers?" Cloe asked, back at her table.

"I think that'll be perfect," Sasha agreed. "Much more than that could get hard for me to supervise."

"Sasha, you're not in charge here!" Cloe

complained.

"No—I know—that's not what I meant," Sasha protested.

The others just shook their heads at her. They loved Sasha's take-charge attitude, but sometimes she took her role as the most organized of her friends a little too seriously.

The bell jangled loudly, summoning the students back to their classes.

"See you after school!" Meygan called, heading off with Vinessa as the others waved goodbye.

"Ugh, I have a review for my Biology final now," Cloe groaned.

"I have the same thing in Chemistry," Jade added.

"Psychology final prep for me," Yasmin declared.

"And I'll be getting ready for my Math

final," Sasha said. "Yep, should be a fun day."

"Maybe finals week wasn't the ideal time to make over an entire shelter, huh?" Jade asked.

"We're always up for a challenge, aren't we?" Sasha asked.

"Totally!" her best friends agreed cheerfully.

They grabbed their bags, dumped their trays, and headed off to class, too energized by their latest project to feel very worried about all their upcoming tests. After all, they knew they could do anything when they put their minds to it!

CHAPTER 6

"Instead of all these cages, could we create more of an open play area?" Cloe asked Ms. Fiske at the shelter that afternoon.

"That sounds great," Ms. Fiske agreed. "Though we should probably keep a few smaller areas for some of our shyer pets."

"Oh, of course," Cloe replied.

She showed the shelter's director her sketches for the main cat and dog play areas, with pens branching off from each for animals that needed to be on their own.

"This looks incredible, Cloe," Ms. Fiske exclaimed. "But you know we can't afford something like this, right?"

"Don't worry," Sasha told her. "Bowwow Meow Magazine has agreed to sponsor the event and donate materials." She glanced at Cloe's elaborate plans and added, "Though we still might need to scale back a little from the plans Cloe has here."

She noticed Cloe's disappointed look and added, "But we'll make as much of this happen as we possibly can."

"Thanks, Sash," Cloe said gratefully.

The boys showed up then, along with Meygan and Vinessa, and together the nine friends started repainting the exterior with the paint Cameron's shop teacher had donated to their cause. Soon

©MGA

it was a gleaming cream color that made it look fresh and fabulous.

Ms. Leland showed up with her camera crew to catch some of the makeover on tape.

"Good work!" she shouted.

"Tomorrow we'll do the bright-blue contrasting trim," Jade announced.

"It looks gorgeous already," Ms. Fiske declared. "And I can't believe how fast you did it!"

"It's easy when we all work together," Yasmin explained. "But now we've really got to get home and do some studying. See you tomorrow!"

"Do you really think we'll have time to get everything finished?" Cloe asked worriedly as she drove Yasmin home.

"We'll manage somehow," Yasmin replied. "We always do."

The next morning, the girls hosted their first segment on the school's TV station, featuring a sweet little grey cat named Velvet. Jade held Velvet while Sasha told viewers about her profile, explaining how the poor kitty had been left all by herself in the shopping mall's parking lot.

Then Yasmin told viewers about the shelter, Jade explained about the makeover they were doing, and Cloe urged everyone to come out to the pet show.

"You'll meet tons of cute animals like Velvet here, who just need a loving family to take care of them!" she announced.

Velvet batted happily at a toy that Yasmin dangled in front of her, purring loudly from all the attention.

"This cat is so lonely!" Jade said after the segment was over. "I feel terrible for her."

"But I'm sure being in our Pet Spotlight will help her find a new home," Yasmin reassured her.

"She really deserves a home," Jade said. "She's the sweetest cat ever!"

"Okay, hand her over," Sasha insisted. "I have to get her back to the shelter."

"If I have to..." Jade gave Velvet one last scratch behind the ears and stroke on the cheek, then gave the kitten to Sasha.

Sasha drove Velvet back to the shelter and, by the time she got there, a whole line of people were waiting to adopt Velvet.

"Apparently your classmates called their parents after they saw your show and said they had to have that kitty," Ms. Fiske explained.

"Well, I guess Velvet goes to the first arrival," Sasha replied. "But luckily there are lots of other adorable kittens inside!"

Ms. Fiske was so overwhelmed by the crowd of potential new pet owners that Sasha stuck around for a while to help her. Half an hour later, ten people had gone home with new cats, and Sasha had to jet back to school to make it to her third-hour class.

That afternoon, Sasha made an announcement on the school radio station about the upcoming event, and the town radio station promoted it all day long. By the time Sasha, Jade, Cloe, Yasmin and their friends returned to the shelter after school, it was completely swamped with people.

"You girls sure are keeping me busy!" Ms. Fiske called when she saw her new helpers arrive. "We've found homes for fifteen more animals since you left, Sasha!"

Meygan, Vinessa, and the guys went to help Ms. Fiske with the crowd while Cloe, Jade,

Sasha and Yasmin looked on in amazement.

"At this rate, we aren't going to have any animals left for the show," Jade declared.

"I think we could include recently adopted pets too, couldn't we?" Yasmin suggested. "I mean, we don't want to discourage people from getting a pet now because they want to make sure they'll have a shot at owning a prize-winning pet, or something."

"Sure, if people want to doll up their dogs and cats and bring them in, I think that's totally cool," Cloe agreed. "As long as they got them at the shelter, of course."

"I'm glad you said that, because I really want to enter Aspen," Yasmin said.

"Do you really think that's fair, since she's the mascot and all?" Sasha asked.

"Hey, I didn't ask for her to be the mascot," Yasmin complained. "And I think she should get a shot in the show, too."

"I pretty much had to make her the mascot to calm you down," Cloe protested.

"That's not fair!" Yasmin shouted.

"Anyway, we'll all be too busy running the event to look after our own animals," Sasha added, trying to calm down her friend.

"You wouldn't be saying that if you had a pet of your own you wanted to enter," Yasmin replied, her arms crossed over her chest. "Look, I'm taking a lot of time away from Aspen to help all these other animals, but she is the reason we all got involved in this, and I think it's only fair if she gets to be in the show."

"I think she's right," Jade added. "I mean, if it means that much to Yas, why shouldn't she get to

©MGA

show off her adorable puppy?"

Yasmin shot Sasha and Cloe a defiant look. Finally, Sasha sighed and looked away.

"You know, I guess it isn't that big of a deal. But you will still help us with all the other animals at the show, right?"

"Of course!" Yasmin cried. "It's just—you know, Aspen had as hard a life as any of these other abandoned pets, and I want her to have her chance to shine, just like the chance we're giving all of them."

Cloe looked at her friend thoughtfully for a moment before agreeing, "That does seem fair."

"Okay, guys, I know we're all stressed about getting all of this done, but are we finished bickering yet?" Jade asked. "Because we kind of have a lot of work to do."

Jade was always so calm that the others

depended on her to spread her chill vibe around.

"Right—back to work," Sasha announced.

"Good to know things are back to normal," Yasmin said with a grin.

They headed inside, where Ms. Fiske took a moment away from all the adoption paperwork she was doing to show the girls the shipment they'd gotten from Bowwow Meow.

"I couldn't believe how many boxes the delivery man brought in!" she told them, leading them to the shelter's back room.

"Whoa," Jade gasped.

There were piles of cat and dog beds, blankets, collars, cat furniture, cat toys, dog bones—everything Ms. Tanaka at the magazine had promised, and more.

"Now this I can work with!" exclaimed Jade.

"And they also sent a quite sizable check,"

Ms. Fiske continued. "So it looks like we can pull off all of your renovation ideas."

She showed the check to the girls and they all oohed and aahed in amazement.

"We've gotten the school to donate so many supplies that there's no way we'll need all of this cash," Sasha declared. "But it'll make a nice donation to the shelter, don't you think?"

"I won't argue with that!" Ms. Fiske exclaimed, shaking her head. "The animals and I feel so lucky to have you girls on our side!"

"We're just glad to be able to help," Yasmin said modestly.

The girls got to work painting the trim outside, then started outfitting Cloe's new doggie play area, carting out empty cages to make room for a comfy, open space.

While they were working, Cloe noticed a darling brown-and-cream-colored puppy who kept following her around while she worked, wagging its tail eagerly.

"Aren't you the sweetest?" she asked, scooping up the little cutie. She kept taking breaks from her redecorating to pet the puppy, and soon her friends started to notice.

"Who's your new friend?" Vinessa asked, sitting down beside Cloe to grab a drink of water.

"I don't know her name, but she's as soft as my favorite cashmere sweater," Cloe replied. She paused, staring into the puppy's big brown eyes, then added, "I don't think I can stand to leave her here!"

She called her parents and got their permission to adopt the puppy.

"They said they knew this would happen, with all the time I was spending over here," she admitted to her friends. "But they totally went for it!"

"And what are you going to name her?" Yasmin asked, scratching behind the puppy's ears.

"I think I have to call her Cashmere," Cloe said. "I mean, isn't her fur just the softest?"

"It sure is," Yasmin agreed. "And now Aspen has her new friend to play with!"

"Ooh, and we can take them to puppy-training classes together, and go to the dog park together, and have puppy play dates," Cloe squealed. "This'll be the most fun ever!"

"And we can get them both ready for the dog show together," Yasmin added. "You do want to enter her, don't you?"

"Of course!" Cloe cried. Then she looked at her friend sheepishly and said, "Huh, it is different when you have one of your own, isn't it?"

"Yep," Yasmin replied. "And I'm so glad you're getting the chance to try it out for yourself!"

Before they knew it, it was time to head home again.

"I love it here," Cloe gushed on the way out, her brand-new puppy cradled in her arms. "I don't know why we never hung out here before!"

"It's not exactly the best hangout spot," Sasha pointed out.

"But by the time we're finished with it, it will be!" Jade declared.

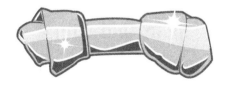

CHAPTER 7

All week long, the girls alternated studying for tests with sprucing up the Stilesville Animal Shelter and doing promotions for the pet show.

"Thank goodness we got that killer History final out of the way early," Cloe said as they arrived at the pet shelter the Saturday after their last finals—and the official first day of summer vacation. "I would never have been able to handle it by the end of this week!"

"Did you survive the rest of your finals?" Jade asked.

"Yep," Cloe replied. "You?"

"I think so," Jade said with a shrug.

"Cloe, you look tired," Yasmin told her best friend. "Is Cashmere sleeping through the night yet?"

"Nope," Cloe replied. "Is Aspen?"

"Not yet," Yasmin admitted. "But I'm still hopeful."

"I can't believe you wrote that awesome article for the school paper on zero sleep," Jade said.

"And the piece you did for the town newspaper was even better!" Sasha added.

"Writing during all this craziness has got to be a sign of true talent!"

"We always knew Yasmin was incredibly talented," Cloe said, putting her arm around her friend.

"Just like my best friends," Yasmin replied with a smile.

The girls shared a group hug, then tackled the shelter redesign once more. They had completely repainted the interiors and taken out all the cages, creating a big, open area for the cats and another one for the dogs, with a couple of smaller, glass-walled enclosures for the pets that needed their own space.

"No more bars for these pets!" Cloe declared, scoping out their handiwork. She was thrilled that they had been able to bring her ideas to life!

The girls looked around, taking in the cats all sprawled over piles of cushions, enjoying scratching posts and dangling toys, and chasing each other up and down and around various levels of carpeted cat furniture. Then they headed over to visit the dogs, who were nestled in doggy beds or cheerfully chasing balls, gnawing on rawhide dog bones or rolling around on the floor together. All the animals seemed to be having a fantastic time.

"They just love the company," Yasmin murmured. "That was what always made me so sad–that they were all so isolated. But now none of these little guys has to be alone."

"It really does look spectacular," Jade said, "and the pets look way happier than they did when we started. But now I think it's time for the finishing touches."

With her friends' help, Jade got to work adding curtains made from the pretty polka-dotted fabric her home-ec teacher had given her, arranging fluffy new cushions that her classmates had made, and adding toys from the Bowwow Meow stash at strategic points around each play area. The girls tried different configurations of the cat furniture until it looked just right, and fastened a sparkling new collar onto each and every pet.

"It seems like there were a lot more pets when we started last week," Cloe said once they had accessorized each of the animals.

"There were—Ms. Fiske told me that with every day of announcements, more and more people have come here to adopt," Sasha replied. "In the past week, they've found homes for over sixty cats and dogs!"

"All because of us?" Yasmin asked, amazed.

"Pretty much," Sasha confirmed. "She said they're usually lucky to send ten pets home in a week."

"So how many do we have left?" Jade scanned the dog room, then darted into the cat room and did a quick count. "Looks like only thirty—can that be right?"

"I think so," Yasmin agreed. "Well, that makes the pet makeover part way easier!"

"Exactly," Sasha said.

"Let's get started!" Cloe exclaimed.

The girls bathed all the dogs, lathering them up in a big tub at the back of the shelter. They laughed as the fifteen puppies wiggled and splashed in the water, occasionally leaping out and trailing soap bubbles down the hallway with them.

After they had rinsed them all off, they hand-dried them, and then brushed them until their coats shone. All the dogs looked brand new, their fur gleaming in the sunlight in the play yard out back. The girls had built that, too, to make sure the dogs could get some fresh air during their time at the shelter.

"They look so proud of themselves!" Jade declared.

And it was true—all of the puppies were sitting up straighter and wagging their tails as if to say, "Look at me!"

Sasha seemed especially impressed by a tiny, short-haired tan puppy with pointy, perky ears.

"I know they're all cute, but I really think this one is the cutest," she announced.

She crouched down on the floor to pet the puppy's head, and soon the dog rolled over so Sasha could rub her belly.

"Uh-oh, I think someone else has caught the puppy bug," Cloe said knowingly.

"Hey, I'll admit it," Sasha replied. "I already asked my parents if I could adopt one, just in case something like this happened. And luckily, they said okay."

"So is this the one for you?" Yasmin asked.

"Definitely," Sasha answered. At the sound of her voice, the puppy hopped up, yipped excitedly, then ran in circles around her. "I mean, check out how feisty she is!"

"Hmm, that does seem like a perfect fit," Jade agreed with a laugh.

"And do you have a brilliant name for her yet?" Cloe wanted to know.

"I was thinking I'd call her Tango," Sasha replied.

The puppy barked in response, and the girls burst out in giggles.

"I think you got that one right," Yasmin told her.

"Yeah, she seems to approve," Sasha said. "Besides, I can already tell she's got some cool

©MGA

dance moves—just like me!"

Sasha scooped up her puppy and twirled around with her like they were grooving on the dance floor.

"How cute!" Cloe cooed.

"Okay, Jade, when are you joining the puppy club?" Yasmin wanted to know.

"I don't know, guys," said Jade. "I mean, most people are either cat people or dog people. And I'm most definitely a cat person."

"But that doesn't mean you couldn't love a sweet little puppy, if the right one came along," Cloe insisted.

"Well...there is this fluffy black-and-white puppy that's kind of stolen my heart," Jade admitted.

"Really?" Sasha asked excitedly, still cuddling her new pet. "Which one is it?"

"Come here, Mocha!" Jade called, and a

short-legged puppy with long, flowing ears scurried over to her.

"I can't believe you were acting like you didn't even want one when you'd named her already!" Cloe said accusingly.

"I couldn't help it!" Jade replied. "It's the perfect name—she looks just like a café mocha, my favorite morning drink! And she kept licking my hand and wanting to play and...well, I'm hooked."

"Does this mean you're a dog person now?" Yasmin teased.

"No way!" Jade declared. "In fact, I'm adopting a cat, too."

"You always have to outdo the rest of us, don't you?" Sasha shook her finger at Jade jokingly.

Jade just shrugged. "I do what I can. So do you want to meet my cat or not?"

The girls headed over to the cat room, where Jade picked up a fluffy black cat with a white diamond on her chest.

"Aww, you'll have a matching cat-and-dog set," Yasmin said. "So what's this one's name? Espresso?"

"Don't be silly," Jade replied. "Actually, her name is Java."

"Too cute!" Cloe declared.

"Well, I'm glad you're such a cat lover," Sasha told Jade. "Because that means you get to lead us in giving all the cats their baths. And you know how much cats love water!"

"Oh, lucky me," Jade sighed, heading for the bathtub with her kitten in her arms. "You cats are gonna love me."

Her new kitten purred happily, and even stayed calm during her bath.

"You really are the perfect cat!" Jade told

Java. "Let's see if your friends can manage to behave themselves, too."

She grabbed her friends to help her bathe the other cats. Many of the kitties wailed when their paws touched the water and kept trying to climb out of the tub, but by the end they were all fluffed up and glossy. Even the ones who'd looked the most miserable during their baths seemed happy with their new looks.

"What can I say?" Jade told her friends. "Cats love to look good!"

CHAPTER 8

The girls spent the first few days of their summer vacation prepping the pets for their big debut, and the days flew by. And all week, more pets kept getting adopted—though of course new ones came into the shelter every day.

Cloe's gorgeous poster for the event was plastered all over town, and people were constantly calling the shelter to reserve tickets.

"We're going to raise a ton of money for the shelter with admission to the show alone!" Cloe declared.

Cameron, Dylan and Koby had built a stage in the shelter's newly revamped lobby, where the show would take place, and the girls started running dress rehearsals on it. They wanted the pets to feel totally comfortable once they were onstage so they could show off to their best advantage.

The dogs would walk down the runway on leashes that matched their glam new collars, so they needed to get used to

©MGA

following commands while on their leashes. The cats would be carried down the runway on plump, posh pillows, and needed practice at staying put while they were being held. The girls went over the routine with each pet over and over again until every animal seemed totally chill about the process.

A couple of days before the show, the girls gave the puppies haircuts and styled their fur to make them even cuter.

"Nobody's gonna be able to resist these little guys," Jade announced, admiring her makeover handiwork.

They still had tons of details to finalize for the event itself, so the girls spent a lot of time on planning that last week. Dylan agreed to DJ, and Sasha worked on creating a totally cool playlist for him. Cameron offered to do lights, and Jade gave him the lighting cues. And Vinessa and Meygan agreed to help the other girls walk the pets down the runway.

Cloe planned a menu and bought refreshments, while Yasmin lined up judges— Mr. Siegel from the paper, Ms. Leland from the TV station, and Ms. Clark from the radio station all agreed to help out. Even Ms. Tanaka from Bowwow Meow Magazine was flying in for the event, and said she'd be honored to serve as a judge!

"Well, at least we know the media will be covering the event—I just hope they can take some time out from judging to write something down," Jade joked.

The girls would be showing all the animals that were still at the shelter, while the ones that had already been adopted would be shown by their new owners. Yasmin was collecting entry forms with pictures and a brief description so she could make up the perfect award for every single pet.

Although the 'Best in Show' award would be a real competition, for everything else, Yasmin wanted to make sure every animal was a winner. She spent a ton of time coming up with creative prizes for all of them, and Jade was busy making ribbons to keep up with Yasmin's contestant list.

"Whoa, look at these guys," Yasmin gasped the day before the show, holding out a snapshot of two truly hideous dogs. They were grayish-brown, scrawny, and wrinkled, and in the picture they had their long noses stuck up in the air. "Someone with a really big heart must have adopted these two."

"It says they're twins," Jade said, reading the entry form. "Their names are Huffy and Puffy and they enjoy winning, looking down on other dogs, and being spoiled. Wow, they sound like a real treat."

"Do you think I could get away with a

'snottiest' award?" Yasmin asked.

"Hmm, maybe not. What about 'most sure of themselves'?" Jade suggested.

"But that seems too nice for these two!" Yasmin protested. "But I shouldn't be so mean. Just look at them—these guys must've had a tough life. What about 'most unusual'?"

"That'll work!" Jade agreed with a laugh. "I've never seen a dog like these two before!"

"Let's just hope we never do again," Yasmin sighed.

"We'll get to see them at the pet show," Jade reminded her. "Won't that be a thrill?"

"Well, there'll be plenty of cute pets to distract us," Yasmin told her. "Aww, like this one!" She held up a shot of a fuzzy orange cat and showed it to her friend.

"Oh, I remember him from our first visit to the shelter—I'm so glad he found a home!"

Jade exclaimed.

"It will be cool to see all the pets we've helped so far with their new owners," Yasmin said. "It'll be a big, happy reunion!"

"Totally," Jade agreed. "Okay, I'm gonna go finalize my stage design." Gesturing at the pile of brightly colored ribbons beside Yasmin, she added, "I think you should have enough ribbons now, right?"

"Definitely," Yasmin replied, glancing up from her stack of entry forms. "Have fun decorating!"

"I always do!" Jade said with a jaunty wave.

She darted to the lobby, where Sasha was setting up the DJ stand and Cloe was practicing her lines.

"How's it coming,

©MGA

girls?" Jade asked her friends.

"I keep testing the music on the pets, and I can't find anything that doesn't scare the cats or make the dogs howl," Sasha complained. She had her new dog, Tango, at her side, along with several other cats and dogs from the shelter. "Well, except for easy listening, but that won't exactly work for strutting down the runway."

"So what are we going to do?" Jade asked.

"Hey, my music library is vast—I'll just keep trying until I find something that works for them," Sasha replied.

"I'm sure you will, Bunny Boo," Jade told her with a grin. "What about you, Cloe?"

"My lines all sound stupid!" Cloe moaned. "Do you think we could get Yasmin up here for a rewrite?"

"Why didn't you just have her write them in

the first place?" Sasha inquired.

"I don't know...I guess I thought it would sound more natural if I came up with them myself," Cloe admitted. "But this doesn't sound natural at all!"

"I'm sure Yasmin can spruce it up," Jade said. "Why don't you ask her to help?"

Cloe headed to the office at the back of the shelter, where Yasmin was camped out, and her friend started fixing the script right away.

Back on the stage, Jade was draping fabric in the show's pink-and-black polka-dotted color scheme to make the lobby totally glam.

"Jade, that looks gorgeous!" Sasha exclaimed.

"I think the pets will look really cute on this backdrop," Jade explained. "It should be good for all different fur colors."

"I love that you think about things like

that," Sasha told her.

"And I love that you think about things like which tunes would be the perfect ones to bring the event to life," Jade added.

"Guess we're a good team, huh?" Sasha asked. She played another track, and suddenly the pets all perked up, bobbing their heads to the beat.

"I think you've found it!" Jade declared.

"This is totally rockin'!" Sasha cried. "You animals have awesome taste in music."

"I knew there was a reason we liked them," Jade said.

Cloe ran back out with Yasmin following behind her.

"I love this song!" Cloe exclaimed. She and her best friends started grooving to the music as the animals yipped and mewed along. "Where did you find it?"

"Oh, it's a new indie artist I heard downtown," Sasha told her. "But it's really the pets who picked it out."

"Music genius pets, huh?" Yasmin asked. "We should've put that on the poster!"

"It's okay, I'll make an announcement at the show," Cloe said seriously.

"Good, because I think that's going to be a huge help in finding these guys new homes," Sasha replied. The girls all laughed as they kept dancing to the pets' new favorite song.

"Everything looks fabulous," Jade declared. "But there's just one thing missing."

"What?" Sasha cried. "What'd I forget?"

"Well, we're all going onstage tomorrow, right?" Jade asked. The girls nodded. "And do any of us have the perfect new outfit to wear?"

"Oh no!" Cloe wailed. "I have no clue what

I'm wearing tomorrow!"

"Luckily, our local shopping mall can solve that problem," Jade interrupted. "Shopping anyone?"

"Always!" her best friends exclaimed.

CHAPTER 9

The girls hit the mall in search of outfits that would coordinate with Jade's color scheme. They rang up Vinessa and Meygan to meet them there, since they would be going onstage too.

"I just don't have a picture in my head of what cute dog-walking attire would be," Cloe admitted once they had all gathered at the mall.

"I'm thinking long ruffled skirts and tank tops," Jade, their style guru, suggested. "How's that sound?"

"Fabulous," Yasmin replied. "You always have the hippest style ideas. But do you think we'll be able to find the right looks?"

"Not a problem," Jade assured her.

"What's our first stop?" Meygan asked.

"Unique Boutique?" Cloe suggested. "I always find the coolest skirts there."

"Good call," Jade agreed.

The girls descended on the store, and soon each of them had armfuls of frilly, flirty skirts. They dashed into the dressing room and started modeling the skirts for each other.

"Cloe, I love that!" Vinessa squealed, checking out Cloe's knee-length polka-dotted skirt with a white lacy hem. "It's totally sweet!"

"Thanks, Vinessa," Cloe replied. "But look at you—you've got a whole outfit already!"

She glanced admiringly at Vinessa's dark-pink sleeveless top with a ribbon tie, paired

©MGA

with a chocolate-brown skirt with contrasting black trim.

"I know—I wanted to scope out the other stores before I picked something, but I'm crazy about this ensemble," Vinessa admitted.

"Then go for it!" Jade exclaimed, stepping out in a ruffled pink skirt that fell to her ankles.

"I think you should go for that!" Yasmin called as she emerged in a natural-tone skirt with a leopard-print pattern, plus a hot-pink tank top with rhinestones studding the neckline.

"You found a whole outfit already, too?" Cloe gasped. "Oh, man, I am so behind!"

"Nah, it just means we get to keep on shopping," Sasha told her, striking a pose in a pink flower-print skirt.

"Don't you look cute?" Meygan cried,

appearing from her changing stall in a multi-tiered black skirt and black-and-pink striped sleeveless shirt.

"We all look cute!" Jade declared. "Okay girls, are we ready to hit the next store?"

"You know it!" Cloe said. "I've got to complete this outfit!"

The girls changed back into their own clothes, paid for their purchases, then headed for Over the Tops to find some hip tanks.

"I have to have this!" Cloe exclaimed, grabbing a white tank top that read "My Dog Rocks."

"Too cool," Sasha agreed, snagging a simple, petal-pink sleeveless shirt.

"Love it!" Jade cried, spotting Sasha's top. "In fact, I think I'll get the same one in black!"

"Wait, does that mean we're finished already?" Meygan asked, sounding disappointed. "That was the shortest shopping trip ever!"

"No way!" Sasha replied. "We've still got to accessorize."

The girls hurried to the checkout counter, and then it was on to Etc., their fave accessory store.

"I think we need some chic belts to really complete our outfits," Jade announced, holding up a classic-looking gold-chain belt.

"I'm digging the belt idea," Meygan agreed, choosing a beaded one with a jaunty pink rose clipped onto it.

Sasha picked out a sparkly belt with a heart-shaped buckle while Yasmin grabbed a black belt with a round, rhinestone-studded buckle.

"I think I'll stick with this purse," Vinessa told her

©MGA

friends, gazing admiringly at a light-colored plaid purse with white trim.

"I'm with you," Cloe added, going for a hot-pink handbag. "Ooh, and this gold dog-tag necklace, too!"

"What a perfect accessory for a dog show!" Vinessa gushed.

"I know, am I clever or what?" Cloe replied with a grin.

The girls were about to pay for their new finds when Jade shouted, "Wait! No!"

Her friends turned to stare at her. "Are you okay, Jade?" Yasmin asked.

"Shoes! We forgot shoes!" she wailed.

"Well, disaster averted, my friend," Sasha teased, heading for the shoe racks.

Soon each girl had found a super-cute new pair of shoes: brown pumps for Vinessa, pink for Sasha, and black for Meygan. Yasmin chose black heels with a tiny pink bow at the toe, Cloe picked pink, polka-dotted heels, and Jade went for pale pink with hot-pink accents at the heel and toe.

"Now is it safe to leave the store?" Cloe wanted to know.

"I think so," Jade confirmed.

"All right, girls, rest up tonight—we have a big day tomorrow!" Sasha reminded her friends in the parking lot as they all loaded their shopping bags into their cars.

"We'll be ready for it," Yasmin promised.

CHAPTER 10

The girls got up early the next day to do a local news piece about the pet show, and the segment went spectacularly well.

"This'll run tonight," the producer, Ms. Leland, promised.

Then they stopped into the radio station and did a quick chat on the morning show. Ms. Clark at the station told them their spot was awesome. Sasha was feeling good, but by the time they reached the shelter, Cloe was already frantic.

"Are you sure everything's ready?" she asked anxiously. "I can't believe the day of the show is here already!"

"Let me worry about that," Sasha replied. "After all, keeping things running smoothly is my specialty."

"So does that mean everything's ready?" Cloe insisted.

"Of course it is," Jade told her. "With Sasha in charge, what are you worried about?"

"Here, let's go through my checklist," Sasha suggested. "The refreshments are all set to go, right?" Cloe nodded.

"The decorations look spectacular, the pets are all groomed and have tons of practice on the runway, the music is totally hot and Dylan's all set to spin the records, the lighting design will be dazzling and Cam knows all the cues, Koby is running the ticket booth, the judges have the lists of contestants and all the prizes, the media is coming and we have a huge audience lined up, too."

The girls stared at her, stunned. "What? Did I miss something?"

"No, I think that's everything," Yasmin declared. "I mean, literally, everything. Feel better, Cloe?"

"Absolutely," Cloe agreed. "Sorry I ever doubted you, Sash!"

"No worries," Sasha said. "I needed to check everything off my list, anyway."

"Hey, ladies!" Vinessa called, bursting through the shelter's front door with Meygan at her side.

Vinessa was looking especially polished, decked out in her new threads with her pale blonde hair pulled back in a long, sleek ponytail. The other girls were in their chic new outfits too, but had left their hair long and loose and softly curled at the ends.

"Oh good, the crew's all here!" Sasha

cheered. "Because here come the contestants!"

She pointed outside, where proud owners were arriving with their newly adopted friends. Sasha and Meygan started checking them in, while Cloe and Yasmin went over the final order the pets would be coming out in, and Jade and Vinessa hurried to the cat and dog rooms to prep the homeless pets for their big debut. They fluffed up the animals' fur and fastened pretty bows to the girl puppies' ears.

"Perfect!" Jade declared.

"Girls!" Sasha dashed in and cried. "You'll never believe it, but the Tweevils are out there!"

"What?" Jade gasped. "Why?"

"They snuck their snooty purebreds in under fake names," Sasha explained.

The girls hurried to the lobby, and Jade

marched right up to the Tweevils.

"We told you, this is for adopted pets only. Your overpriced pooches don't exactly qualify."

"Too late now," Kirstee snapped.

"Yeah, we aren't leaving!" Kaycee declared.

"Guys, it'll kind of ruin our lineup if we pull any of the pets now," Yasmin whispered. "I think we have to let them stay."

"Fine," Jade muttered. "It's not like their weird little dogs will do well, anyway."

"Places, everyone!" Cloe called out. "Girls, line up backstage with your first pets. We'll start with a round of dogs, then bring out the cats for the next round. Does everyone know which pets they're escorting?"

©MGA

"Yep," the girls chorused.

They darted backstage, and Sasha cued Koby at the front door to let in the audience. Peeking out moments later, the girls were thrilled to see a huge crowd of people clustered around the stage.

"Are the judges ready?" Meygan asked.

"Yep, I've got them all set up," Yasmin replied. "I'm so psyched that such important people are judging this show!"

Sasha rushed over and exclaimed, "Let's get this party started!"

She cued the lights and music, and Cloe stepped up to the microphone.

"I'm thrilled to welcome all of you to the first annual Stilesville Precious Paws Pet Show, sponsored by Bowwow Meow Magazine!" The crowd cheered loudly as Cloe continued, "You'll think these kitties are the cat's meow, and we're sure you'll fall in puppy love with these dogs! And remember, most of these pets are still up for adoption—check your programs to find out which of our contestants are still looking for homes of their own."

The girls strutted out with their first batch of puppies as Cloe announced, "Let's hear it for Jade, Meygan, Sasha, Vinessa, and Yasmin, with some of Stilesville's sweetest puppies ever!"

The audience adored all the animals— except for the Tweevils' dogs, Muffy and Buffy, who, with their strange posing and preening, just seemed to confuse the crowd.

By the end of the night, every pet had a prize—even Muffy and Buffy with their 'Most Unusual' award. Then the judges named their finalists for 'Best in Show'. Aspen, Mocha, Cashmere, and Tango had all made the cut, along with Java and Velvet, their first featured pet from the school's morning show.

Meygan took over the microphone so Cloe could show off her puppy, while Vinessa carried Velvet onto the stage.

"How could you not pick Muffy and Buffy?" Kaycee shouted.

"Yeah!" Kirstee yelled. "They were the classiest dogs in the whole show!"

"That may be true," Ms. Tanaka replied, "but they weren't the best. Sorry."

"Humph!" the Tweevils scoffed, stomping out of the shelter.

The judges shook their heads, returning their attention to the final tally sheets.

"And the winner is..." Ms. Tanaka began.

©MGA

The girls clutched one another's hands!

"...Aspen!" announced Ms. Tanaka. "This sweet little puppy will be featured on the cover of Bowwow Meow as the Precious Paws Best in Show!"

"Oh my gosh!" Yasmin squealed. She bent down to hug her puppy, then pulled all of her friends into a group hug. "I wish all our puppies could've won," she whispered to the girls.

"Nah," Cloe replied. "Aspen started all this, and it's only fair that she gets to finish it. You and Aspen totally deserve the prize!"

Yasmin rushed to the judge's table, where Mr. Siegel draped the giant 'Best in Show' ribbon Jade had made around Aspen's neck. Ms. Tanaka snapped pictures for the magazine, while Ms. Leland's cameras rolled.

"I'll have my story on the whole show in to you by tomorrow," Yasmin told Mr. Siegel.

"And I'm sure it'll be great," he replied.

"I want you all to join me for a follow-up piece on our show tomorrow," Ms. Leland declared.

"We'd love to!" Yasmin squealed.

"And you have to come on my radio show again, too," Ms. Clark added.

"Absolutely," Yasmin agreed.

Ms. Fiske rushed over to them and grabbed the judges' microphone.

"Every single pet was adopted tonight," she announced. The crowd cheered wildly as she continued, "And we raised enough money to keep all of our little friends fed for many years to come."

She waved Cloe, Jade, and Sasha over, and the girls hurried to join Ms. Fiske at the judges' table. Ms. Fiske slung her arms around the girls and finished, "I want to thank these young ladies for saving so many animals through their creativity, determination, and compassion. The pets and I owe a lot to Cloe, Jade, Sasha, and Yasmin."

The audience applauded, while the pets barked and meowed happily. Ms. Tanaka leaned in to snap a group shot.

"What can I say?" Cloe declared. "We're always happy to help."

"Especially when it involves adorable, helpless pets," Yasmin added, picking up Aspen and nuzzling her head.

"Especially then!" Cloe agreed.

Read more about the Bratz in
these other awesome books!

Pixie Power
Spring Break Safari
Diamond Road Trip

BRATZ
Magazine

the magazine for girls with a PASSION for fashion!

ALL THE LATEST BRATZ & CELEBRITY NEWS!

ALL THE BEST FASHION TIPS & ADVICE!

COOL FEATURES, COMPETITIONS, POSTERS & MORE!

U.K. Customers get 1 issue free!
13 issues for only £29.25
Order online www.titanmagazines.co.uk/bratz
or call 0870 428 8206 (Quoting ref BRZPA1)

U.S. Customers Save 35%!
6 issues for only $19.50
Order online www.titanmagazines.com/bratz
or call 1 877 363 1310 (Quoting ref BRZPA2)